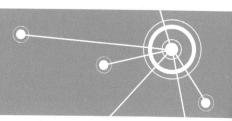

THE COMMON CORE

Clarifying Expectations for Teachers & Students

ENGLISH LANGUAGE ARTS

Grade 8

**Created and Presented by
Align, Assess, Achieve**

Mc Graw Hill Education

★ Align, Assess, Achieve, LLC

Align, Assess, Achieve; *The Common Core: Clarifying Expectations for Teachers &*
Students. Grade 8

STEM McGraw-Hill is committed to providing instructional materials in Science,
Technology, Engineering, and Mathematics (STEM) that give all students a solid
foundation, one that prepares them for college and careers in the 21st century.

Send all inquiries to:
McGraw-Hill Education
STEM Learning Solutions Center
8787 Orion Place
Columbus, OH 43240

ISBN: 978-007-662961-9
MHID: 0-07-662961-9

Printed in the United States of America.

3 4 5 6 7 8 9 QGL 17 16 15 14 13 12

Our mission is to provide educational resources
that enable students to become the problem solvers
of the 21st century and inspire them to explore
careers within Science, Technology, Engineering,
and Mathematics (STEM) related fields.

Acknowledgements

This book integrates the Common Core State Standards – a framework for educating students to be competitive at an international level – with well-researched instructional planning strategies for achieving the goals of the CCSS. Our work is rooted in the thinking of brilliant educators, such as Grant Wiggins, Jay McTighe, and Rick Stiggins, and enriched by our work with a great number of inspiring teachers, administrators, and parents. We hope this book provides a meaningful contribution to the ongoing conversation around educating lifelong, passionate learners.

We would like to thank many talented contributors who helped create *The Common Core: Clarifying Expectations for Teachers and Students.* Our authors, Lani Meyers and Mindy Holmes, for their intelligence, persistence, and love of teaching; Graphic Designer Thomas Davis, for his creative talents and good nature through many trials; Editors, Laura Gage and Dr. Teresa Dempsey, for their educational insights and encouragement; Director of book editing and production Josh Steskal, for his feedback, organization, and unwavering patience; Our spouses, Andrew Bainbridge and Tawnya Holman, who believe in our mission and have, through their unconditional support and love, encouraged us to take risks and grow.

Katy Bainbridge
Bob Holman
Co-Founders
Align, Assess, Achieve, LLC

Executive Editors: *Katy Bainbridge and Bob Holman*
Authors: *Mindy Holmes and Lani Meyers*
Contributing Authors: *Teresa Dempsey, Katy Bainbridge and Bob Holman*
Graphic Design & Layout: *Thomas Davis; thomasanceldesign.com*
Director of Book Editing & Production: *Josh Steskal*

Introduction

Purpose

The Common Core State Standards (CCSS) provide educators across the nation with a shared vision for student achievement. They also provide a shared challenge: how to interpret the standards and use them in a meaningful way? Clarifying the Common Core was designed to facilitate the transition to the CCSS at the district, building, and classroom level.

Organization

Clarifying the Common Core presents content from two sources: the CCSS and Align, Assess, Achieve. Content from the CCSS is located in the top section of each page and includes the strand, CCR, and grade level standard. The second section of each page contains content created by Align, Assess, Achieve – Enduring Understandings, Essential Questions, Suggested Learning Targets, and Vocabulary. The black bar at the bottom of the page contains the CCSS standard identifier. A sample page can be found in the next section.

Planning for Instruction and Assessment

This book was created to foster meaningful instruction of the CCSS. This requires planning both quality instruction and assessment. Designing and using quality assessments is key to high-quality instruction (Stiggins et al.). Assessment should accurately measure the intended learning and should inform further instruction. This is only possible when teachers and students have a clear vision of the intended learning. When planning instruction it helps to ask two questions, "Where am I taking my students?" and "How will we get there?" The first question refers to the big picture and is addressed with **Enduring Understandings** and **Essential Questions**. The second question points to the instructional process and is addressed by **Learning Targets**.

Where Am I Taking My Students?

When planning, it is useful to think about the larger, lasting instructional concepts as **Enduring Understandings**. Enduring Understandings are rooted in multiple units of instruction throughout the year and are often utilized K-12. These concepts represent the lasting understandings that transcend your content. Enduring Understandings serve as the ultimate goal of a teacher's instructional planning. Although tempting to share with students initially, we do not recommend telling students the Enduring Understanding in advance. Rather, Enduring Understandings are developed through meaningful

Essential Questions work in concert with Enduring Understandings to ignite student curiosity. These questions help students delve deeper and make connections between the concepts and the content they are learning. Essential Questions are designed with the student in mind and do not have an easy answer; rather, they are used to spark inquiry into the deeper meanings (Wiggins and McTighe). Therefore, we advocate frequent use of Essential Questions with students. It is sometimes helpful to think of the Enduring Understanding as the answer to the Essential Question.

How Will We Get There?

If Enduring Understandings and Essential Questions represent the larger, conceptual ideas, then what guides the learning of specific knowledge, reasoning, and skills? These are achieved by using **Learning Targets**. Learning Targets represent a logical, student friendly progression of teaching and learning. Targets are the scaffolding students climb as they progress towards deeper meaning.

There are four types of learning targets, based on what students are asked to do: knowledge, reasoning/understanding, skill, and product (Stiggins et al.). When selecting Learning Targets, teachers need to ask, "What is the goal of instruction?" After answering this question, select the target or targets that align to the instructional goal.

Instructional Goal	*Target Type*	*Key Verbs*
Recall basic information and facts	Knowledge (K)	Name, identify, describe
Think and develop an understanding	Reasoning/ Understanding (R)	Explain, compare and contrast, predict
Apply knowledge and reasoning	Skill (S)	Use, solve, calculate
Synthesize to create original work	Product (P)	Create, write, present

Adapted from Stiggins et al. *Classroom Assessment for Student Learning.* (Portland: ETS, 2006). Print.

Keep in mind that the Enduring Understandings, Essential Questions, and Learning Targets in this book are suggestions. Modify and combine the content as necessary to meet your instructional needs. Quality instruction consists of clear expectations, ongoing assessment, and effective feedback. Taken together, these promote meaningful instruction that facilitates student mastery of the Common Core State Standards.

References

Stiggins, Rick, Jan Chappuis, Judy Arter, and Steve Chappuis. *Classroom Assessment for Student Learning.* 2nd. Portland, OR: ETS, 2006.

Wiggins, Grant, and Jay McTighe. *Understanding by Design, Expanded 2nd Edition.* 2nd. Alexandria, VA: ASCD, 2005.

Page Organization

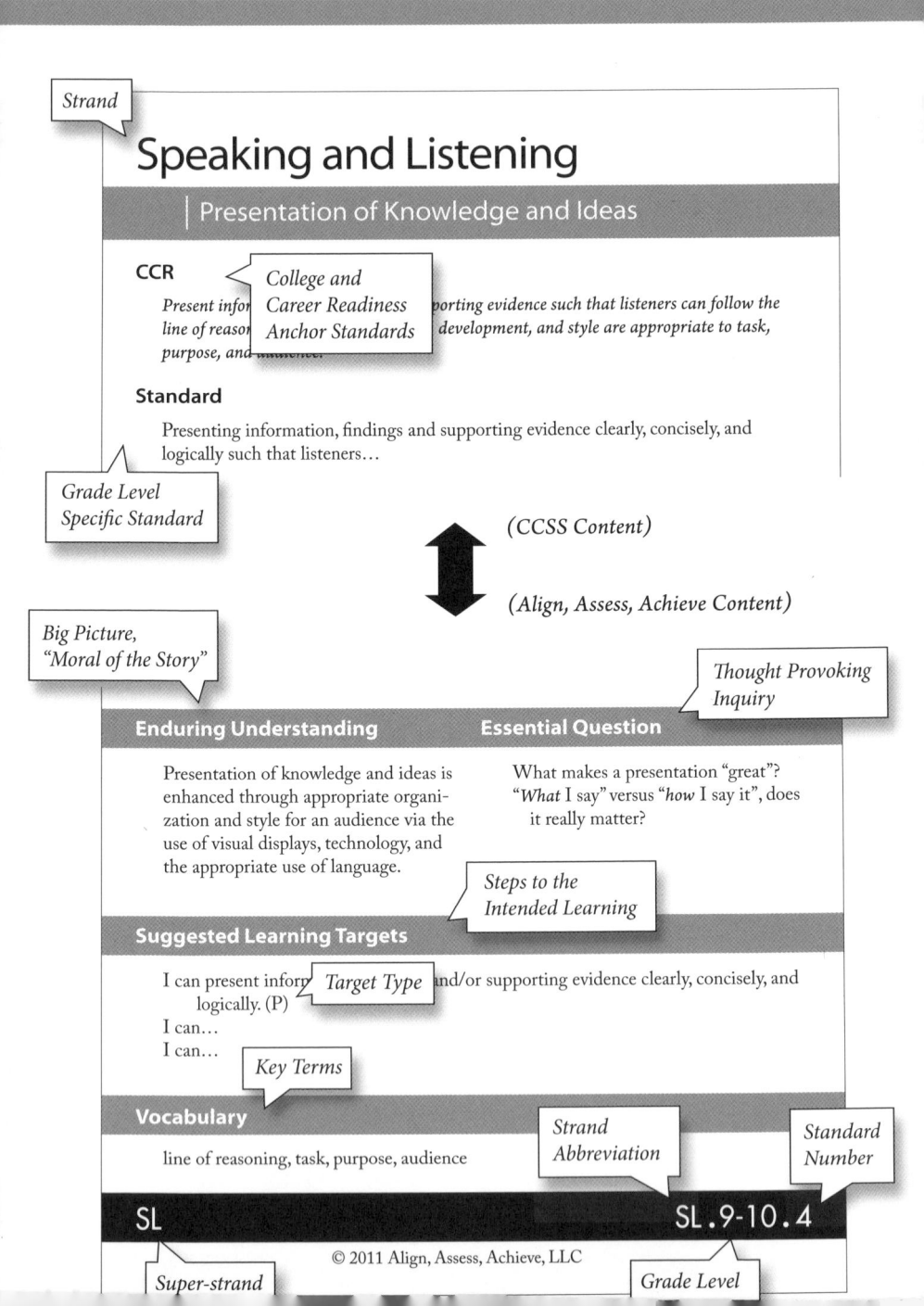

Strand

Speaking and Listening

Presentation of Knowledge and Ideas

CCR

College and Career Readiness Anchor Standards

Present infor... ...orting evidence such that listeners can follow the line of reaso... ...development, and style are appropriate to task, purpose, and...

Standard

Presenting information, findings and supporting evidence clearly, concisely, and logically such that listeners...

Grade Level Specific Standard

(CCSS Content)

(Align, Assess, Achieve Content)

Big Picture, "Moral of the Story"

Thought Provoking Inquiry

Enduring Understanding

Presentation of knowledge and ideas is enhanced through appropriate organization and style for an audience via the use of visual displays, technology, and the appropriate use of language.

Essential Question

What makes a presentation "great"? "*What* I say" versus "*how* I say it", does it really matter?

Steps to the Intended Learning

Suggested Learning Targets

I can present infor... *Target Type* ...nd/or supporting evidence clearly, concisely, and logically. (P)
I can...
I can...

Key Terms

Vocabulary

line of reasoning, task, purpose, audience

Strand Abbreviation

Standard Number

SL

SL.9-10.4

Super-strand

Grade Level

Literature

CCR

Read closely to determine what the text says explicitly and to make logical inferences from it; cite specific textual evidence when writing or speaking to support conclusions drawn from the text.

Standard

Cite the textual evidence that most strongly supports an analysis of what the text says explicitly as well as inferences drawn from the text.

Enduring Understanding

Effective readers use a variety of strategies to make sense of the ideas and details presented in text.

Essential Questions

What do good readers do?
Am I clear about what I just read?
How do I know?

Suggested Learning Targets

I can define textual evidence (a "word for word" support format). (K)
I can define inference and explain how a reader uses textual evidence to reach a logical conclusion ("based on what I've read, it's most likely true that..."). (R)
I can read closely and find answers explicitly in text (right there answers) and answers that require an inference. (S)
I can analyze an author's words and determine the textual evidence that most strongly supports both explicit and inferential questions. (R)

Vocabulary

textual evidence, analyze, inference, explicit

R

RL.8.1

Literature

CCR

Determine central ideas or themes of a text and analyze their development; summarize the key supporting details and ideas.

Standard

Determine a theme or central idea of a text and analyze its development over the course of the text, including its relationship to the characters, setting, and plot; provide an objective summary of the text.

Enduring Understanding

Effective readers use a variety of strategies to make sense of key ideas and details presented in text.

Essential Questions

What do good readers do?
Am I clear about what I just read?
How do I know?

Suggested Learning Targets

I can define theme (a central idea or lesson the author is revealing – *Honesty is the best policy.*). (K)
I can analyze plot (the events that happen) to determine a theme (author's overall message). (R)
I can determine how key events, characters' actions and interactions, and setting develop over the course of the text to contribute to the theme. (R)
I can define summary (a shortened version of the text that states its key points). (K)
I can compose an objective summary stating the key points of the text without adding my own opinions or feelings. (P)

Vocabulary

theme, summary, objective, central idea, opinion

R   RL.8.2

Literature

CCR

Analyze how and why individuals, events, and ideas develop and interact over the course of a text.

Standard

Analyze how particular lines of dialogue or incidents in a story or drama propel the action, reveal aspects of a character, or provoke a decision.

Enduring Understanding	Essential Questions
Effective readers use a variety of strategies to make sense of the ideas and details presented in text.	What do good readers do? Am I clear about what I just read? How do I know?

Suggested Learning Targets

- I can identify particular lines of dialogue in a story or drama that propel the action, reveal aspects of a character, or provoke a decision. (K)
- I can analyze how a particular line of dialogue in a story or drama propels the action (e.g., *Sasha said, "Josh is the worst singer in the school choir." This leads to the action of Josh crying in the corner.*). (R)
- I can analyze how a particular line of dialogue in a story or drama reveals aspects of a character (e.g., *Because Sasha said, "Josh is the worst singer in the school choir," the reader realizes that Sasha is either jealous, hateful, or vengeful.*). (R)
- I can analyze how a particular line of dialogue in a story or drama provokes a decision (e.g., *Because Sasha said, "Josh is the worst singer in the school choir," Josh decides to quit the choir.*). (R)
- I can identify particular incidents in a story or drama that propel the action, reveal aspects of a character, or provoke a decision. (K)

(continued on next page)

Vocabulary

dialogue, analyze

R

RL.8.3

Literature

CCR

Analyze how and why individuals, events, and ideas develop and interact over the course of a text.

Standard

Analyze how particular lines of dialogue or incidents in a story or drama propel the action, reveal aspects of a character, or provoke a decision.

Suggested Learning Targets

(continued from previous page)

I can analyze how a particular incident in a story or drama propels the action (e.g., *Lance steals a copy of the midterm exam, which leads to Lance getting a perfect score on the exam.*). (R)

I can analyze how a particular incident in a story or drama reveals aspects of the character (e.g., *Because Lance steals a copy of the exam, the reader realizes Lance is dishonest.*). (R)

I can analyze how a particular incident in a story or drama provokes a decision (e.g., *Because Lance steals a copy of the exam, he begins to feel guilty and decides to tell the teacher.*). (R)

I can recognize how making a change to one line of dialogue or one incident of a story or drama could affect the actions, aspects of a character, or decisions. (R)

R

RL.8.3 *(cont.)*

Literature

CCR

Interpret words and phrases as they are used in a text, including determining technical, connotative, and figurative meanings, and analyze how specific word choices shape meaning or tone.

Standard

Determine the meaning of words and phrases as they are used in a text, including figurative and connotative meanings; analyze the impact of specific word choices on meaning and tone, including analogies or allusions to other texts.

Enduring Understanding

Analyzing texts for structure, purpose, and viewpoint allows an effective reader to gain insight and strengthen understanding.

Essential Questions

Author's choice: Why does it matter? What makes a story a "great" story?

Suggested Learning Targets

I can define and identify various forms of figurative language (e.g., simile, metaphor, hyperbole, personification, alliteration, assonance, onomatopoeia). (K)

I can distinguish between literal language (it means exactly what it says) and figurative language (sometimes what you say is not exactly what you mean). (K)

I can recognize the difference between denotative meanings (all words have a dictionary definition) and connotative meanings (some words carry feeling). (K)

I can analyze why authors choose specific words to evoke a particular meaning or tone. (R)

I can define and identify analogies (comparisons between two things that are similar) and allusions (indirect references to other texts). (K)

I can analyze why authors choose to include particular analogies (e.g., *In a speech by Martin Luther King Jr., he compares coming to the capital to cashing a check.*) and/or allusions (e.g., *In a speech by Martin Luther King Jr., he alludes to the Declaration of Independence, The Gettysburg Address, a spiritual song, etc.*). (R)

Vocabulary

figurative language, denotative meaning, analogy, literal language, connotative meaning, allusion

R   RL.8.4

Literature

CCR

Analyze the structure of texts, including how specific sentences, paragraphs, and larger portions of the text (e.g., a section, chapter, scene, or stanza) relate to each other and the whole.

Standard

Compare and contrast the structure of two or more texts and analyze how the differing structure of each text contributes to its meaning and style.

Enduring Understanding

Analyzing texts for structure, purpose, and viewpoint allows an effective reader to gain insight and strengthen understanding.

Essential Questions

Author's choice: Why does it matter? What makes a story a "great" story?

Suggested Learning Targets

I can compare (analyze the similarities) and contrast (analyze the differences) the structures found in two or more texts. (R)

I can analyze the differing structures of two or more text and determine how the differences affect the overall meaning and style of each text. (R)

I can infer why an author chose to present his/her text using a particular structure. (R)

Vocabulary

compare, contrast, text structure, infer

R

RL.8.5

Literature

CCR

Assess how point of view or purpose shapes the content and style of a text.

Standard

Analyze how differences in the points of view of the characters and the audience or reader (e.g., created through the use of dramatic irony) create such effects as suspense or humor.

Enduring Understanding

Analyzing texts for structure, purpose, and viewpoint allows an effective reader to gain insight and strengthen understanding.

Essential Questions

Author's choice: Why does it matter? What makes a story a "great" story?

Suggested Learning Targets

I can recognize how an author develops the points of view of characters and narrators by revealing thoughts, feelings, actions, and spoken words. (K)

I can recognize how the points of view of characters and audience or reader can be different. (K)

I can analyze how differing points of view can create various effects (e.g., dramatic irony – When the audience or reader knows something that the characters do not, the text can be suspenseful or humorous.). (R)

Vocabulary

point of view, dramatic irony, suspense

R   RL.8.6

Literature

CCR

Integrate and evaluate content presented in diverse media and formats, including visually and quantitatively, as well as in words.*

Standard

Analyze the extent to which a filmed or live production of a story or drama stays faithful to or departs from the text or script, evaluating the choices made by the director or actors.

*Please see "Research to Build Knowledge" in Writing and "Comprehension and Collaboration" in Speaking and Listening for additional standards relevant to gathering, assessing, and applying information from print and digital sources.

Enduring Understanding

To gain keener insight into the integration of knowledge and ideas, effective readers analyze and evaluate content, reasoning, and claims in diverse formats.

Essential Questions

In what ways does creative choice impact an audience?
Whose story is it, and why does it matter?

Suggested Learning Targets

I can compare (analyze the similarities) and contrast (analyze the differences) a filmed or live production of a story or drama and the original text or script. (R)
I can identify various techniques (e.g., lighting, camera angles) used in a filmed or live production of a story or drama. (K)
I can analyze how various techniques used in a filmed or live production of a story or drama can add to or change the experience of the audience. (R)
I can evaluate why directors choose to stay faithful to or depart from a text and/or script. (R)

Vocabulary

compare, contrast, analyze

Integration of Knowledge and Ideas

CCR

Delineate and evaluate the argument and specific claims in a text, including the validity of the reasoning as well as the relevance and sufficiency of the evidence.

Standard

(Not applicable to literature)

(No Common Core State Standard #8 for Reading and Literature)

Literature

CCR

Analyze how two or more texts address similar themes or topics in order to build knowledge or to compare the approaches the authors take.

Standard

Analyze how a modern work of fiction draws on themes, patterns of events, or character types from myths, traditional stories, or religious works such as the Bible, including describing how the material is rendered new.

Enduring Understanding

To gain keener insight into the integration of knowledge and ideas, effective readers analyze and evaluate content, reasoning, and claims in diverse formats.

Essential Questions

In what ways does creative choice impact an audience?
Whose story is it, and why does it matter?

Suggested Learning Targets

I can identify themes, patterns of events, or characters from myths, traditional stories, or religious works that are found in modern works of fiction (e.g., *Traditional fairy tales are often re-created with more modern problems, settings, and characters.*). (K)

I can compare (analyze the similarities) and contrast (analyze the differences) traditional themes, events, or characters to modern interpretations of the same themes, events, or characters. (R)

I can analyze and describe how authors if modern works of fiction draw on traditional themes, events, or characters and render them new. (R)

Vocabulary

theme, modern work of fiction, compare, contrast, render

Literature

CCR

Read and comprehend complex literary and informational texts independently and proficiently.

Standard

By the end of the year, read and comprehend literature, including stories, dramas, and poems, at the high end of grades 6–8 text complexity band independently and proficiently.

Enduring Understanding

Students who are college and career ready read and interpret a variety of complex texts with confidence and independence.

Essential Questions

What do good readers do?
Am I clear about what I just read?
How do I know?

Suggested Learning Targets

I can closely read complex grade level texts. (S)
I can reread a text to find more information or clarify ideas. (S)
I can use reading strategies (e.g., ask questions, make connections, take notes, make inferences, visualize, re-read) to help me understand difficult complex text. (S)

Vocabulary

reading strategy, comprehension

R   RL.8.10

Informational Text

Key Ideas and Details

CCR

Read closely to determine what the text says explicitly and to make logical inferences from it; cite specific textual evidence when writing or speaking to support conclusions drawn from the text.

Standard

Cite the textual evidence that most strongly supports an analysis of what the text says explicitly as well as inferences drawn from the text.

Enduring Understanding

Effective readers use a variety of strategies to make sense of key ideas and details presented in text.

Essential Questions

What do good readers do?
Am I clear about what I just read?
How do I know?

Suggested Learning Targets

I can define textual evidence ("word for word" support). (K)
I can define inference and explain how a reader uses textual evidence to reach a logical conclusion ("based on what I've read, it's most likely true that..."). (R)
I can read closely and find answers explicitly in text (right there answers) and answers that require an inference. (S)
I can analyze an author's words and determine the textual evidence that most strongly supports both explicit and inferential questions. (R)

Vocabulary

textual evidence, analyze, inference, explicit

R   RI.8.1

Informational Text

CCR

Determine central ideas or themes of a text and analyze their development; summarize the key supporting details and ideas.

Standard

Determine a central idea of a text and analyze its development over the course of the text, including its relationship to supporting ideas; provide an objective summary of the text.

Enduring Understanding

Effective readers use a variety of strategies to make sense of key ideas and details presented in text.

Essential Questions

What do good readers do?
Am I clear about what I just read?
How do I know?

Suggested Learning Targets

I can define central idea (main point in a piece of writing). (K)
I can determine how an author's use of details conveys (makes known) two or more central ideas in a text. (R)
I can analyze how supporting ideas contribute to the development of central ideas over the course of a text. (R)
I can define summary (a shortened version of the text that states its key points). (K)
I can compose an objective summary stating the key points of the text without adding my own opinions or feelings. (P)

Vocabulary

central idea, supporting idea, summary, objective

R   RI.8.2

Informational Text

CCR

Analyze how and why individuals, events, and ideas develop and interact over the course of a text.

Standard

Analyze how a text makes connections among and distinctions between individuals, ideas, or events (e.g., through comparisons, analogies, or categories).

Enduring Understanding	Essential Questions
Effective readers use a variety of strategies to make sense of key ideas and details presented in text.	What do good readers do? Am I clear about what I just read? How do I know?

Suggested Learning Targets

I can explain how the individuals, events, and/or ideas in a text affect one another. (K)

I can analyze connections and distinctions between individuals, events, and/or ideas in a text. (R)

I can analyze how an author makes connections and distinctions between individuals, ideas, or events through comparisons (e.g., *The Underground Railroad and the Jewish Resistance Movement*), analogies (e.g., *One-part-per-billion is equal to one sheet in a roll of toilet paper stretching from New York to London.*), or categories (e.g., *Leaders of Change – Rosa Parks, Mahatma Gandhi, Mother Teresa, Henry Ford*). (R)

Vocabulary

individual, event, idea, connection, distinction

Informational Text

Craft and Structure

CCR

Interpret words and phrases as they are used in a text, including determining technical, connotative, and figurative meanings, and analyze how specific word choices shape meaning or tone.

Standard

Determine the meaning of words and phrases as they are used in a text, including figurative, connotative, and technical meanings; analyze the impact of specific word choices on meaning and tone, including analogies or allusions to other texts.

Enduring Understanding	Essential Questions
Analyzing texts for structure, purpose, and viewpoint allows an effective reader to gain insight and strengthen understanding.	Author's choice: Why does it matter? What makes a story a "great" story?

Suggested Learning Targets

- I can define and identify various forms of figurative language (e.g., simile, metaphor, hyperbole, personification, alliteration, onomatopoeia). (K)
- I can distinguish between literal language (it means exactly what it says) and figurative language (sometimes what you say is not exactly what you mean). (K)
- I can recognize the difference between denotative meanings (all words have a dictionary definition) and connotative meanings (some words carry feeling). (K)
- I can recognize words that have technical meaning and understand their purpose in a specific text (e.g., "stem" in an article about flowers versus "stem" in an article about cell research). (R)
- I can analyze why authors choose words and phrases, including analogies (comparisons between two things that are similar) and allusions (indirect references to other texts), to set the tone and create an overall meaning and mood for the reader. (R)

Vocabulary

figurative language, literal language, denotative meaning, connotative meaning, technical meaning, tone, mood, analogy, allusion

R

RI.8.4

Informational Text

CCR

Analyze the structure of texts, including how specific sentences, paragraphs, and larger portions of the text (e.g., a section, chapter, scene, or stanza) relate to each other and the whole.

Standard

Analyze in detail the structure of a specific paragraph in a text, including the role of particular sentences in developing and refining a key concept.

Enduring Understanding

Analyzing texts for structure, purpose, and viewpoint allows an effective reader to gain insight and strengthen understanding.

Essential Questions

Author's choice: Why does it matter? What makes a story a "great" story?

Suggested Learning Targets

I can analyze the structure of a specific paragraph in a text and determine how this paragraph helps to develop or refine a key concept. (R)
I can analyze and explain how the role of particular sentences (e.g., topic sentence, supporting detail) help to develop and refine the author's key concept. (R)

Vocabulary

refine

R   RI.8.5

Informational Text

CCR

Assess how point of view or purpose shapes the content and style of a text.

Standard

Determine an author's point of view or purpose in a text and analyze how the author acknowledges and responds to conflicting evidence or viewpoints.

Enduring Understanding

Analyzing texts for structure, purpose, and viewpoint allows an effective reader to gain insight and strengthen understanding.

Essential Questions

Author's choice: Why does it matter?
What makes a story a "great" story?

Suggested Learning Targets

I can define point of view as how the author feels about the situation/topic of a text. (K)

I can determine an author's point of view (*What do I know about the author's opinions, values, and/or beliefs?*) and explain his/her purpose for writing the text. (R)

I can analyze how an author acknowledges and responds to conflicting evidence or viewpoints (*How does the author respond? Does he/she use information, evidence, statistics, etc. to strengthen his/her own viewpoint?*). (R)

Vocabulary

point of view, purpose, analyze

R   RI.8.6

Informational Text

CCR

Integrate and evaluate content presented in diverse media and formats, including visually and quantitatively, as well as in words.*

Standard

Evaluate the advantages and disadvantages of using different mediums (e.g., print or digital text, video, multimedia) to present a particular topic or idea.

*Please see "Research to Build Knowledge" in Writing and "Comprehension and Collaboration" in Speaking and Listening for additional standards relevant to gathering, assessing, and applying information from print and digital sources.

Enduring Understanding

To gain keener insight into the integration of knowledge and ideas, effective readers analyze and evaluate content, reasoning, and claims in diverse formats.

Essential Questions

In what ways does creative choice impact an audience?
Whose story is it, and why does it matter?

Suggested Learning Targets

I can explain how informational text is presented in different mediums (e.g., audio, video, multimedia). (K)
I can analyze a particular topic or idea and explore how authors use different mediums of presentation (e.g., video diary, PowerPoint, visual display). (R)
I can evaluate the advantages and disadvantages of presenting a topic or idea in different mediums. (R)

Vocabulary

medium, analyze, evaluate

Informational Text

CCR

Delineate and evaluate the argument and specific claims in a text, including the validity of the reasoning as well as the relevance and sufficiency of the evidence.

Standard

Delineate and evaluate the argument and specific claims in a text, assessing whether the reasoning is sound and the evidence is relevant and sufficient; recognize when irrelevant evidence is introduced.

Enduring Understanding

To gain keener insight into the integration of knowledge and ideas, effective readers analyze and evaluate content, reasoning, and claims in diverse formats.

Essential Questions

In what ways does creative choice impact an audience?
Whose story is it, and why does it matter?

Suggested Learning Targets

I can identify the side of an argument an author presents in a text. (K)
I can determine the credibility of the author and his/her purpose (who wrote it, when it was written, and why it was written). (R)
I can identify claims that are supported by fact(s) and those that are opinion(s). (K)
I can recognize when an author introduces irrelevant evidence (unrelated or unnecessary evidence) to his/her argument. (R)
I can delineate and evaluate an argument using the evidence an author provides and determine if the evidence provided is relevant and sufficient enough to support the claim. (R)

Vocabulary

delineate, claim, relevant, argument, fact, sufficient, credibility, opinion

R

RI.8.8

Informational Text

CCR

Analyze how two or more texts address similar themes or topics in order to build knowledge or to compare the approaches the authors take.

Standard

Analyze a case in which two or more texts provide conflicting information on the same topic and identify where the texts disagree on matters of fact or interpretation.

Enduring Understanding

To gain keener insight into the integration of knowledge and ideas, effective readers analyze and evaluate content, reasoning, and claims in diverse formats.

Essential Questions

In what ways does creative choice impact an audience?

Whose story is it, and why does it matter?

Suggested Learning Targets

I can recognize how two or more texts can provide conflicting information on the same topic. (K)

I can analyze how authors interpret and emphasize different evidence when writing about the same topic. (R)

I can compare (analyze the similarities) how two or more texts communicate the same topic. (R)

I can contrast (analyze the differences) how two or more texts communicate the same topic. (R)

I can identify where two or more texts on the same topic disagree on matters of fact or interpretation. (R)

I can describe how one author's interpretation of a topic can be different from another author's depending on how the facts are interpreted. (R)

Vocabulary

point of view, compare, contrast, interpretation, evidence

R   RI.8.9

Informational Text

CCR

Read and comprehend complex literary and informational texts independently and proficiently.

Standard

By the end of the year, read and comprehend literary nonfiction at the high end of the grades 6–8 text complexity band independently and proficiently.

Enduring Understanding

Students who are college and career ready read and interpret a variety of complex texts with confidence and independence.

Essential Questions

What do good readers do?
Am I clear about what I just read?
How do I know?

Suggested Learning Targets

I can closely read complex grade level texts. (S)
I can reread a text to find more information or clarify ideas. (S)
I can use reading strategies (e.g ., ask questions, make connections, take notes, make inferences, visualize, re-read) to help me understand difficult complex text. (S)

Vocabulary

reading strategy, comprehension

R   RI.8.10

Writing

CCR

Write arguments to support claims in an analysis of substantive topics or texts, using valid reasoning and relevant and sufficient evidence.

Standard

Write arguments to support claims with clear reasons and relevant evidence.

a. Introduce claim(s), acknowledge and distinguish the claim(s) from alternate or opposing claims, and organize the reasons and evidence logically.
b. Support claim(s) with logical reasoning and relevant evidence, using accurate, credible sources and demonstrating an understanding of the topic or text.
c. Use words, phrases, and clauses to create cohesion and clarify the relationships among claim(s), counterclaims, reasons, and evidence.
d. Establish and maintain a formal style.
e. Provide a concluding statement or section that follows from and supports the argument presented.

*These broad types of writing include many subgenres. See Appendix A for definitions of key writing types.

Enduring Understanding

Writing should be purposely focused, detailed, organized, and sequenced in a way that clearly communicates the ideas to the reader.

Essential Questions

What do good writers do?
What's my purpose and how do I develop it?

Suggested Learning Targets

I can identify a topic that causes or has caused a debate in society. (K)
I can choose a side of the argument and identify reasons that support my choice. (R)
I can determine the credibility of a source (who wrote it, when it was written, and why it was written) and the accuracy of the details presented in the source. (R)
I can support my argument with textual evidence ("word for word" support) found in credible sources. (R)
I can acknowledge counterclaims (opposing claims) in my argument. (K)
I can present my argument in a formal style that included an introduction, supporting details with transitions, and provide a concluding statement/section that supports my argument. (P)

Vocabulary

debate, counterclaim, transition, argument, evidence, claim, credible source

Writing

CCR

Write informative/explanatory texts to examine and convey complex ideas and information clearly and accurately through the effective selection, organization, and analysis of content.

Standard

Write informative/explanatory texts to examine a topic and convey ideas, concepts, and information through the selection, organization, and analysis of relevant content.

a. Introduce a topic clearly, previewing what is to follow; organize ideas, concepts, and information into broader categories; include formatting (e.g., headings), graphics (e.g., charts, tables), and multimedia when useful to aiding comprehension.
b. Develop the topic with relevant, well-chosen facts, definitions, concrete details, quotations, or other information and examples.
c. Use appropriate and varied transitions to create cohesion and clarify the relationships among ideas and concepts.
d. Use precise language and domain-specific vocabulary to inform about or explain the topic.
e. Establish and maintain a formal style.
f. Provide a concluding statement or section that follows from and supports the information or explanation presented.

These broad types of writing include many subgenres. See Appendix A for definitions of key writing types.

Enduring Understanding	Essential Questions
Writing should be purposely focused, detailed, organized, and sequenced in a way that clearly communicates the ideas to the reader.	What do good writers do? What's my purpose and how do I develop it?

Suggested Learning Targets

I can select a topic and identify and gather relevant information (e.g., well-chosen facts, definitions, details, quotations, examples) to share with my audience. (R)

(continued on next page)

Vocabulary

organizational structures, formatting structures, transitions, cohesion

W   W.8.2

Writing

CCR

Write informative/explanatory texts to examine and convey complex ideas and information clearly and accurately through the effective selection, organization, and analysis of content.

Standard

Write informative/explanatory texts to examine a topic and convey ideas, concepts, and information through the selection, organization, and analysis of relevant content.

  a. Introduce a topic clearly, previewing what is to follow; organize ideas, concepts, and information into broader categories; include formatting (e.g., headings), graphics (e.g., charts, tables), and multimedia when useful to aiding comprehension.
  b. Develop the topic with relevant, well-chosen facts, definitions, concrete details, quotations, or other information and examples.
  c. Use appropriate and varied transitions to create cohesion and clarify the relationships among ideas and concepts.
  d. Use precise language and domain-specific vocabulary to inform about or explain the topic.
  e. Establish and maintain a formal style.
  f. Provide a concluding statement or section that follows from and supports the information or explanation presented.

*These broad types of writing include many subgenres. See Appendix A for definitions of key writing types.

Suggested Learning Targets

(continued from previous page)

I can define common organizational/formatting structures and determine a structure(s) that will allow me to organize my information best. (K)

I can analyze the information, identify vocabulary specific to my topic, and organize information into broader categories using my chosen structure(s). (R)

I can present my information in a formal style that includes an introduction that previews what is to follow, supporting details, varied transitions (to clarify and create cohesion when I move from one idea to another), and a concluding statement/section that supports the information presented. (P)

Writing

CCR

Write narratives to develop real or imagined experiences or events using effective technique, well-chosen details, and well-structured event sequences.

Standard

Write narratives to develop real or imagined experiences or events using effective technique, relevant descriptive details, and well-structured event sequences.

a. Engage and orient the reader by establishing a context and point of view and introducing a narrator and/or characters; organize an event sequence that unfolds naturally and logically.

b. Use narrative techniques, such as dialogue, pacing, description, and reflection, to develop experiences, events, and/or characters.

c. Use a variety of transition words, phrases, and clauses to convey sequence, signal shifts from one time frame or setting to another, and show the relationships among experiences and events.

d. Use precise words and phrases, relevant descriptive details, and sensory language to capture the action and convey experiences and events.

e. Provide a conclusion that follows from and reflects on the narrated experiences or events.

*These broad types of writing include many subgenres. See Appendix A for definitions of key writing types.

Enduring Understanding

Writing should be purposely focused, detailed, organized, and sequenced in a way that clearly communicates the ideas to the reader.

Essential Questions

What do good writers do?
What's my purpose and how do I develop it?

Suggested Learning Targets

I can define narrative and describe the basic parts of plot (exposition, rising action, climax, falling action, and resolution). (K)

(continued on next page)

Vocabulary

narrative, plot structure (exposition, rising action, climax, falling action, resolution), dialogue, transitions, conclusion

W

W.8.3

Writing

CCR

Write narratives to develop real or imagined experiences or events using effective technique, well-chosen details, and well-structured event sequences.

Standard

Write narratives to develop real or imagined experiences or events using effective technique, relevant descriptive details, and well-structured event sequences.

a. Engage and orient the reader by establishing a context and point of view and introducing a narrator and/or characters; organize an event sequence that unfolds naturally and logically.
b. Use narrative techniques, such as dialogue, pacing, description, and reflection, to develop experiences, events, and/or characters.
c. Use a variety of transition words, phrases, and clauses to convey sequence, signal shifts from one time frame or setting to another, and show the relationships among experiences and events.
d. Use precise words and phrases, relevant descriptive details, and sensory language to capture the action and convey experiences and events.
e. Provide a conclusion that follows from and reflects on the narrated experiences or events.

*These broad types of writing include many subgenres. See Appendix A for definitions of key writing types.

Suggested Learning Targets

(continued from previous page)

I can engage the reader by introducing the narrator (first, second or third person point of view), characters, setting (set the scene), and the event that starts the story in motion. (S)

I can use narrative techniques (dialogue, pacing, description, and reflection) to develop a storyline where one event logically leads to another. (S)

I can use descriptive words and phrases that appeal to the senses, capture the action, and help my reader understand the experiences and events (create mind pictures). (S)

I can signal changes in time and place by using transition words, phrases, and clauses to show relationships among experiences and events. (S)

I can write a logical conclusion that reflects on the experiences/events and provides a sense of closure (ties up all the loose ends and leaves the reader satisfied). (P)

Writing

CCR

Produce clear and coherent writing in which the development, organization, and style are appropriate to task, purpose, and audience.

Standard

Produce clear and coherent writing in which the development, organization, and style are appropriate to task, purpose, and audience. (Grade-specific expectations for writing types are defined in standards 1–3 above.)

Enduring Understanding

Producing clear ideas as a writer involves selecting appropriate style and structure for an audience and is strengthened through revision and technology.

Essential Questions

Writing clearly: What makes a difference?

Final product: What does it take?

Suggested Learning Targets

I can identify the writing style (argument, informative/explanatory, or narrative) that best fits my task, purpose, and audience. (K)

I can use organizational/formatting structures (graphic organizers) to develop my writing ideas. (S)

I can compose a clear and logical piece of writing that demonstrates my understanding of a specific writing style. (P)

Vocabulary

writing style, purpose, task, audience

W

W.8.4

Writing

CCR

Develop and strengthen writing as needed by planning, revising, editing, rewriting, or trying a new approach.

Standard

With some guidance and support from peers and adults, develop and strengthen writing as needed by planning, revising, editing, rewriting, or trying a new approach, focusing on how well purpose and audience have been addressed.

Enduring Understanding	Essential Questions
Producing clear ideas as a writer involves selecting appropriate style and structure for an audience and is strengthened through revision and technology.	Writing clearly: What makes a difference? Final product: What does it take?

Suggested Learning Targets

I can use prewriting strategies to formulate ideas (e.g., graphic organizers, brainstorming, lists). (S)

I can recognize that a well-developed piece of writing requires more than one draft. (K)

I can apply revision strategies (e.g., reading aloud, checking for misunderstandings, adding and deleting details) with the help of others. (S)

I can edit my writing by checking for errors in capitalization, punctuation, grammar, spelling, etc. (S)

I can analyze my writing to determine if my purpose and audience have been fully addressed and revise when necessary. (S)

I can prepare multiple drafts using revisions and edits to develop and strengthen my writing. (S)

I can recognize when revising, editing, and rewriting are not enough, and I need to try a new approach. (R)

Vocabulary

revision strategy, edit, purpose, audience

Writing

CCR

Use technology, including the Internet, to produce and publish writing and to interact and collaborate with others.

Standard

Use technology, including the Internet, to produce and publish writing and present the relationships between information and ideas efficiently as well as to interact and collaborate with others.

Enduring Understanding

Producing clear ideas as a writer involves selecting appropriate style and structure for an audience and is strengthened through revision and technology.

Essential Questions

Writing clearly: What makes a difference?

Final product: What does it take?

Suggested Learning Targets

I can identify technology (e.g., Word, Publisher, PowerPoint) that will help me compose, edit and publish my writing. (K)

I can determine the most efficient technology medium for presenting the relationships between information and ideas (e.g., connecting information I have gathered and my own ideas). (S)

I can use technology to produce and publish my writing. (S)

I can collaborate with peers, teachers, and other experts through technology to enhance my writing. (S)

Vocabulary

publish

W

W.8.6

Writing

CCR

Conduct short as well as more sustained research projects based on focused questions, demonstrating understanding of the subject under investigation.

Standard

Conduct short research projects to answer a question (including a self-generated question), drawing on several sources and generating additional related, focused questions that allow for multiple avenues of exploration.

Enduring Understanding

Effective research presents an answer to a question, demonstrates understanding of the inquiry, and properly cites information from multiple sources.

Essential Questions

What do good researchers do?
"Cut and Paste:" What's the problem?

Suggested Learning Targets

I can define research and distinguish how research differs from other types of writing. (K)

I can focus my research around a central question that is provided or determine my own research worthy question (e.g., *How did Edgar Allan Poe's life experiences influence his writing style?*). (S)

I can choose several sources (e.g., biographies, non-fiction texts, online encyclopedia) and gather information to answer my research question. (R)

I can analyze the information found in my sources and determine if it provides enough support to answer my question. (R)

I can create additional focused questions that relate to my original topic and allow for further investigation. (P)

Vocabulary

research, central question, source

W

W.8.7

Writing

CCR

Gather relevant information from multiple print and digital sources, assess the credibility and accuracy of each source, and integrate the information while avoiding plagiarism.

Standard

Gather relevant information from multiple print and digital sources, using search terms effectively; assess the credibility and accuracy of each source; and quote or paraphrase the data and conclusions of others while avoiding plagiarism and following a standard format for citation.

Enduring Understanding

Effective research presents an answer to a question, demonstrates understanding of the inquiry, and properly cites information from multiple sources.

Essential Questions

What do good researchers do?
"Cut and Paste:" What's the problem?

Suggested Learning Targets

I can determine the credibility and accuracy of a source by reviewing who wrote it, when it was written, and why it was written. (R)

I can use search terms effectively to gather information needed to support my research. (S)

I can define plagiarism (using someone else's words/ideas as my own). (K)

I can determine when my research data or facts must be quoted (directly stated – "word for word") in my writing. (R)

I can avoid plagiarism by paraphrasing (putting in my own words) and/or summarizing my research findings. (S)

I can follow a standard format for citation to create a bibliography for sources that I paraphrased or quoted in my writing. (K)

Vocabulary

credibility, search terms, plagiarism, paraphrase, citation

W

W.8.8

Writing

CCR

Draw evidence from literary or informational texts to support analysis, reflection, and research.

Standard

Draw evidence from literary or informational texts to support analysis, reflection, and research.

a.   Apply *grade 8 Reading standards* to literature (e.g., "Analyze how a modern work of fiction draws on themes, patterns of events, or character types from myths, traditional stories, or religious works such as the Bible, including describing how the material is rendered new").

b.   Apply *grade 8 Reading standards* to literary nonfiction (e.g., "Delineate and evaluate the argument and specific claims in a text, assessing whether the reasoning is sound and the evidence is relevant and sufficient; recognize when irrelevant evidence is introduced").

Enduring Understanding

Effective research presents an answer to a question, demonstrates understanding of the inquiry, and properly cites information from multiple sources.

Essential Questions

What do good researchers do?
"Cut and Paste:" What's the problem?

Suggested Learning Targets

I can define textual evidence ("word for word" support). (K)

I can determine textual evidence that supports my analysis, reflection, and/or research. (R)

I can compose written responses and include textual evidence to strengthen my analysis, reflection, and/or research. (P)

Vocabulary

textual evidence, analysis, reflection, research

Writing

CCR

Write routinely over extended time frames (time for research, reflection, and revision) and shorter time frames (a single sitting or a day or two) for a range of tasks, purposes, and audiences.

Standard

Write routinely over extended time frames (time for research, reflection, and revision) and shorter time frames (a single sitting or a day or two) for a range of discipline-specific tasks, purposes, and audiences.

Enduring Understanding

Effective writers use a variety of formats to communicate ideas appropriate for the audience, task, and time frame.

Essential Questions

Why write?
What do good writers do?

Suggested Learning Targets

I can recognize that different writing tasks (e.g., journal, reflection, research) require varied time frames to complete. (K)
I can determine a writing format/style to fit my task, purpose, and/or audience. (R)
I can write for a variety of reasons (e.g., to inform, to describe, to persuade, to entertain/convey an experience). (P)

Vocabulary

writing format, writing style, task, purpose, audience

W   **W.8.10**

Speaking and Listening

CCR

Prepare for and participate effectively in a range of conversations and collaborations with diverse partners, building on others' ideas and expressing their own clearly and persuasively.

Standard

Engage effectively in a range of collaborative discussions (one-on-one, in groups, and teacher-led) with diverse partners on *grade 8 topics, texts, and issues,* building on others' ideas and expressing their own clearly.

a. Come to discussions prepared, having read or researched material under study; explicitly draw on that preparation by referring to evidence on the topic, text, or issue to probe and reflect on ideas under discussion.

b. Follow rules for collegial discussions and decision-making, track progress toward specific goals and deadlines, and define individual roles as needed.

c. Pose questions that connect the ideas of several speakers and respond to others' questions and comments with relevant evidence, observations, and ideas.

d. Acknowledge new information expressed by others, and, when warranted, qualify or justify their own views in light of the evidence presented.

Enduring Understanding

Comprehension is enhanced through a collaborative process of sharing and evaluating ideas.

Essential Questions

What makes collaboration meaningful? Making meaning from a variety of sources: What will help?

Suggested Learning Targets

I can review and/or research the material(s) to be discussed and determine key points and/or central ideas. (R)

I can create questions and locate key textual evidence to contribute to a discussion on the given topic, text, or issue. (P)

I can define the roles and rules necessary for collaborative discussion. (K)

(continued on next page)

Vocabulary

collaborate, elaborate, integrate, warranted, justify

Speaking and Listening

CCR

Prepare for and participate effectively in a range of conversations and collaborations with diverse partners, building on others' ideas and expressing their own clearly and persuasively.

Standard

Engage effectively in a range of collaborative discussions (one-on-one, in groups, and teacher-led) with diverse partners on *grade 8 topics, texts, and issues,* building on others' ideas and expressing their own clearly.

a. Come to discussions prepared, having read or researched material under study; explicitly draw on that preparation by referring to evidence on the topic, text, or issue to probe and reflect on ideas under discussion.

b. Follow rules for collegial discussions and decision-making, track progress toward specific goals and deadlines, and define individual roles as needed.

c. Pose questions that connect the ideas of several speakers and respond to others' questions and comments with relevant evidence, observations, and ideas.

d. Acknowledge new information expressed by others, and, when warranted, qualify or justify their own views in light of the evidence presented.

Suggested Learning Targets

(continued from previous page)

I can come prepared with key points and textual evidence to contribute to a discussion. (S)

I can participate in a discussion by posing questions that connect the ideas of several speakers, responding to questions, and elaborating on my own ideas and/or the ideas of others. (S)

I can track the progress of a discussion and recognize when the discussion is getting off-topic. (S)

I can make relevant observations and use my ideas and comments to further the discussion. (S)

I can review the key ideas presented in a discussion, integrate them with my own when warranted (appropriate), and justify my own views based on evidence introduced by others. (S)

Speaking and Listening

CCR

Integrate and evaluate information presented in diverse media and formats, including visually, quantitatively, and orally.

Standard

Analyze the purpose of information presented in diverse media and formats (e.g., visually, quantitatively, orally) and evaluate the motives (e.g., social, commercial, political) behind its presentation.

Enduring Understanding

Comprehension is enhanced through a collaborative process of sharing and evaluating ideas.

Essential Questions

What makes collaboration meaningful? Making meaning from a variety of sources: What will help?

Suggested Learning Targets

I can identify various purposes (to inform, to persuade, to describe, to convey an experience) for presenting information to a reader or audience. (K)

I can analyze the information presented in a variety of media and formats (e.g., charts, graphs, tables, websites, speeches) to determine the purpose of the presentation. (R)

I can evaluate the motives behind various presentations. (R)

Vocabulary

media, formats, purpose, motive

Speaking and Listening

CCR

Evaluate a speaker's point of view, reasoning, and use of evidence and rhetoric.

Standard

Delineate a speaker's argument and specific claims, evaluating the soundness of the reasoning and relevance and sufficiency of the evidence and identifying when irrelevant evidence is introduced.

Enduring Understanding

Comprehension is enhanced through a collaborative process of sharing and evaluating ideas.

Essential Questions

What makes collaboration meaningful? Making meaning from a variety of sources: What will help?

Suggested Learning Targets

I can identify the side of an argument a speaker presents. (K)
I can determine the credibility of a speaker and his/her purpose. (R)
I can identify claims that are supported by fact(s) and those that are opinion(s). (K)
I can evaluate if a speaker's argument is reasonable (sound) using evidence he/she provides to support his/her claims. (R)
I can identify if a speaker has introduced irrelevant evidence when presenting his/her claim. (K)
I can determine if a speaker has provided enough relevant evidence to support his/her claim or argument. (R)

Vocabulary

argument, credibility, claim, fact, opinion, relevant evidence, irrelevant evidence

SL

SL.8.3

Speaking and Listening

CCR

Present information, findings, and supporting evidence such that listeners can follow the line of reasoning and the organization, development, and style are appropriate to task, purpose, and audience.

Standard

Present claims and findings, emphasizing salient points in a focused, coherent manner with relevant evidence, sound valid reasoning, and well-chosen details; use appropriate eye contact, adequate volume, and clear pronunciation.

Enduring Understanding

Presentation of knowledge and ideas is enhanced through appropriate organization and style for an audience via the use of visual displays, technology, and the appropriate use of language.

Essential Questions

What makes a presentation "great"?
"What I say" versus "how I say it", does it really matter?

Suggested Learning Targets

I can determine salient (important/key) points and emphasize them when presenting my claims and/or findings. (S)
I can support my claims and/or findings with relevant evidence, sound valid reasoning, and well-chosen details. (S)
I can present my information in a logical sequence using appropriate eye contact, adequate volume, and clear pronunciation. (P)

Vocabulary

salient, claim, finding, relevant evidence

Speaking and Listening

CCR

Make strategic use of digital media and visual displays of data to express information and enhance understanding of presentations.

Standard

Integrate multimedia and visual displays into presentations to clarify information, strengthen claims and evidence, and add interest.

Enduring Understanding

Presentation of knowledge and ideas is enhanced through appropriate organization and style for an audience via the use of visual displays, technology, and the appropriate use of language.

Essential Questions

What makes a presentation "great"?
"What I say" versus "how I say it", does it really matter?

Suggested Learning Targets

I can identify the parts of my presentation, including claims and evidence, that could use clarification, strengthening, and/or additional interest. (K)
I can integrate appropriate media component or visual display to improve my presentation. (S)

Vocabulary

clarification, media component, visual display

SL

SL.8.5

Speaking and Listening

CCR

Adapt speech to a variety of contexts and communicative tasks, demonstrating command of formal English when indicated or appropriate.

Standard

Adapt speech to a variety of contexts and tasks, demonstrating command of formal English when indicated or appropriate. (See grade 8 Language standards 1 and 3 for specific expectations.)

Enduring Understanding

Presentation of knowledge and ideas is enhanced through appropriate organization and style for an audience via the use of visual displays, technology, and the appropriate use of language.

Essential Questions

What makes a presentation "great"? "What I say" versus "how I say it", does it really matter?

Suggested Learning Targets

I can identify various reasons for speaking (e.g., informational, descriptive, formal, informal). (K)

I can determine speaking tasks that will require a formal structure. (R)

I can compose a formal speech that demonstrates a command of grade 8 Language standards. (P)

Vocabulary

formal, informal

Language

CCR

Demonstrate command of the conventions of standard English grammar and usage when writing or speaking.

Standard

Demonstrate command of the conventions of standard English grammar and usage when writing or speaking.

a. Explain the function of verbals (gerunds, participles, infinitives) in general and their function in particular sentences.
b. Form and use verbs in the active and passive voice.
c. Form and use verbs in the indicative, imperative, interrogative, conditional, and subjunctive mood.
d. Recognize and correct inappropriate shifts in verb voice and mood.*

* See ELA CCSS Appendix A, page 31 for Language Progressive Skills.

Enduring Understanding

Effective communication of ideas when speaking or writing relies on the appropriate use of the conventions of language.

Essential Questions

Why do the rules of language matter? Communicating clearly: What does it take?

Suggested Learning Targets

I can define and identify gerund (a verb form that ends in –*ing* and is used as a noun), participle (a verb form that is used as an adjective), and infinitive (forms from the word to together with the base form of a verb; often used as a noun in a sentence). (K)

I can explain the function of gerunds (e.g., *Cooking is my favorite hobby.*), participles (e.g., *The respected teacher won an award.*), and infinitives (e.g., *My team wants to win.*). (K)

(continued on next page)

Vocabulary

gerund, participle, infinitive, active voice, passive voice, indicative mood, imperative mood, interrogative mood, conditional mood, subjunctive mood

L

L.8.1

Language

CCR

Demonstrate command of the conventions of standard English grammar and usage when writing or speaking.

Standard

Demonstrate command of the conventions of standard English grammar and usage when writing or speaking.

a. Explain the function of verbals (gerunds, participles, infinitives) in general and their function in particular sentences.
b. Form and use verbs in the active and passive voice.
c. Form and use verbs in the indicative, imperative, interrogative, conditional, and subjunctive mood.
d. Recognize and correct inappropriate shifts in verb voice and mood.*

* See ELA CCSS Appendix A, page 31 for Language Progressive Skills.

Suggested Learning Targets

(continued from previous page)

I can explain the difference between verbs in the active voice (the subject performs the action of the verb) and the passive voice (the subject receives the action of the verb). (K)

I can create sentences with verbs in the active voice (e.g., *The cat scratched Allina.*) and in the passive voice (e.g., *Allina was scratched by the cat.*). (P)

I can explain the difference between verbs in the indicative mood (verbs are used to express facts or opinions), imperative mood (verbs are used to give orders or make requests), interrogative mood (verbs are used to ask questions), conditional mood (verbs are used to express uncertainty), and subjunctive mood (verbs are used to describe a state contrary to fact). (K)

I can create sentences with verbs in the indicative mood (e.g., *Angie closes the door.*), imperative mood (e.g., *Close the door, Angie!*), interrogative mood (e.g., *Angie will you close the door?*), conditional mood (e.g., *Angie might close the door.*), and subjunctive mood (e.g., *If Angie closes the door, a window may open.*) (P)

I can identify and correct inappropriate shifts in verb voice (e.g., *Whenever Tara sang, our dog barks loudly. SHOULD BE Whenever Tara sings, our dog barks loudly.*). (S)

I can identify and correct inappropriate shifts in verb mood (e.g., *If Jackie was rich, she would buy a mansion. SHOULD BE If Jackie were rich, she would buy a mansion.*). (S)

Language

CCR

Demonstrate command of the conventions of standard English capitalization, punctuation, and spelling when writing.

Standard

Demonstrate command of the conventions of standard English capitalization, punctuation, and spelling when writing.

a. Use punctuation (comma, ellipsis, dash) to indicate a pause or break.
b. Use an ellipsis to indicate an omission.
c. Spell correctly.

Enduring Understanding

Effective communication of ideas when speaking or writing relies on the appropriate use of the conventions of language.

Essential Questions

Why do the rules of language matter? Communicating clearly: What does it take?

Suggested Learning Targets

I can determine when to capitalize words (e.g., proper nouns, "I", first word in a sentence). (K)

I can determine when to use a comma or commas to indicate a pause or a break (e.g., introductory words, direct address, parenthetical elements). (R)

I can determine when to use an ellipsis to indicate a pause or a break (e.g., a pause in the flow of the sentence; *"I'm wondering . . . " Ali said, bemused."*). (R)

I can determine when to use a dash or dashes to indicate a pause or a break (e.g., to show a sudden break or change in thought or speech; *Our friend, Cesar – an expert in paint – told us to always use a primer.*). (S)

I can use an ellipsis to show when words I am quoting are left out in the middle or at the end of a sentence (e.g., *President Mahony said, "Teachers are important . . . to educate our future generations."*). (S)

I can identify misspelled words and use resources to assist me in spelling correctly. (K)

Vocabulary

ellipsis, dash

L   L.8.2

Language

CCR

Apply knowledge of language to understand how language functions in different contexts, to make effective choices for meaning or style, and to comprehend more fully when reading or listening.

Standard

Use knowledge of language and its conventions when writing, speaking, reading, or listening.

a. Use verbs in the active and passive voice and in the conditional and subjunctive mood to achieve particular effects (e.g., emphasizing the actor or the action; expressing uncertainty or describing a state contrary to fact).

Enduring Understanding

Effective readers, writers, and listeners use knowledge of language to make appropriate choices when presenting information and to clarify meaning when reading or listening.

Essential Questions

How does situation affect meaning?
How does author's choice impact an audience?

Suggested Learning Targets

I can explain the difference between verbs in the active voice (the subject performs the action of the verb) and the passive voice (the subject receives the action of the verb). (K)

I can create sentences with verbs in the active voice (e.g., *The cat scratched Allina.*) and in the passive voice (e.g., *Allina was scratched by the cat.*) to achieve a particular effect. (P)

I can explain the difference between verbs in the conditional mood (verbs are used to express uncertainty) and subjunctive mood (verbs are used to describe a state contrary to fact). (K)

I can create sentences with verbs in the conditional mood (e.g., *Angie might close the door.*), and subjunctive mood (e.g., *If Angie closes the door, a window may open.*) to achieve a particular effect. (P)

Vocabulary

active voice, passive voice, conditional mood, subjunctive mood

Language

CCR

Determine or clarify the meaning of unknown and multiple-meaning words and phrases by using context clues, analyzing meaningful word parts, and consulting general and specialized reference materials, as appropriate.

Standard

Determine or clarify the meaning of unknown and multiple-meaning words or phrases based on *grade 8 reading and content*, choosing flexibly from a range of strategies.

a. Use context (e.g., the overall meaning of a sentence or paragraph; a word's position or function in a sentence) as a clue to the meaning of a word or phrase.
b. Use common, grade-appropriate Greek or Latin affixes and roots as clues to the meaning of a word (e.g., *precede, recede, secede*).
c. Consult general and specialized reference materials (e.g., dictionaries, glossaries, thesauruses), both print and digital, to find the pronunciation of a word or determine or clarify its precise meaning or its part of speech.
d. Verify the preliminary determination of the meaning of a word or phrase (e.g., by checking the inferred meaning in context or in a dictionary).

Enduring Understanding

Effective readers and writers use knowledge of the structure and context of language to acquire, clarify, and appropriately use vocabulary.

Essential Questions

When a word doesn't make sense, what can I do?
How do I use what I know to figure out what I don't know?

Suggested Learning Targets

I can infer the meaning of unknown words using context clues (e.g., definitions, synonyms/antonyms, restatements, examples found in surrounding text). (R)
I can recognize and define common Greek and Latin affixes and roots (units of meaning). (K)
I can break down unknown words into units of meaning to infer the definition of the unknown word. (R)
I can verify my inferred meaning of an unknown word by consulting general and specialized reference materials (e.g., dictionaries, glossaries, thesauruses). (K)

Vocabulary

infer, context clues, affix, root, reference material

L   L.8.4

Language

CCR

Demonstrate understanding of word relationships and nuances in word meanings.

Standard

Demonstrate understanding of figurative language, word relationships, and nuances in word meanings.

a. Interpret figures of speech (e.g., verbal irony, puns) in context.
b. Use the relationship between particular words to better understand each of the words.
c. Distinguish among the connotations (associations) of words with similar denotations (definitions) (e.g., *bullheaded, willful, firm, persistent, resolute*).

Enduring Understanding	Essential Questions
Effective readers and writers use knowledge of the structure and context of language to acquire, clarify, and appropriately use vocabulary.	When a word doesn't make sense, what can I do? How do I use what I know to figure out what I don't know?

Suggested Learning Targets

I can define and identify various forms of figurative language (e.g., simile, metaphor, hyperbole, personification, alliteration, onomatopoeia). (K)

I can distinguish between literal language (it means exactly what it says) and figures of speech (sometimes what you say is not exactly what you mean). (K)

I can recognize word relationships and use the relationships to further understand multiple words (e.g., *sympathetic/apathetic*). (S)

I can recognize the difference between denotative meanings (all words have a dictionary definition) and connotative meanings (some words carry feeling). (K)

I can analyze how certain words and phrases that have similar denotations (definitions) can have very different connotations (feelings). (R)

Vocabulary

figure of speech, literal language, word relationships, denotation, connotation

Language

CCR

Acquire and use accurately a range of general academic and domain-specific words and phrases sufficient for reading, writing, speaking, and listening at the college and career readiness level; demonstrate independence in gathering vocabulary knowledge when encountering an unknown term important to comprehension or expression.

Standard

Acquire and use accurately grade-appropriate general academic and domain-specific words and phrases; gather vocabulary knowledge when considering a word or phrase important to comprehension or expression.

Enduring Understanding

Effective readers and writers use knowledge of the structure and context of language to acquire, clarify, and appropriately use vocabulary.

Essential Questions

When a word doesn't make sense, what can I do?
How do I use what I know to figure out what I don't know?

Suggested Learning Targets

I can recognize the difference between general academic words and phrases (Tier Two words are subtle or precise ways to say relatively precise things, e.g., *saunter* instead of *walk*.) and domain-specific words and phrases (Tier Three words are often specific to content knowledge, e.g., *lava, legislature, carburetor*.).* (K)

I can acquire and use grade-appropriate academic and domain-specific words/phrases to increase comprehension and expression. (S)

*Tier One, Tier Two, and Tier Three words are clarified on pages 33-35 of Appendix A in the Common Core Standards.

Vocabulary

general academic words, domain specific words

L

L.8.6